Fact Finders®

The Biggest Battles of the Revolutionary War

by Christopher Forest

Consultant:
Richard Bell
Assistant Professor, Department of History
University of Maryland
College Park, Maryland

CAPSTONE PRESS
a capstone imprint

Fact Finders are published by Capstone Press,
1710 Roe Crest Drive, North Mankato, Minnesota 56003.
www.capstonepub.com

Library of Congress Cataloging-in-Publication Data
Forest, Christopher.
  The biggest battles of the Revolutionary War / by Christopher Forest.
    p. cm. — (Fact finders. The story of the American Revolution)
  Summary: "Describes causes and outcomes of key battles of the Revolutionary
    War"—Provided by publisher.
  Includes bibliographical references and index.
  ISBN 978-1-4296-8429-3 (library binding)
  ISBN 978-1-4296-9282-3 (paperback)
  ISBN 978-1-62065-244-2 (ebook PDF)
  1. United States—History—Revolution, 1775–1783—Campaigns—Juvenile
    literature. I. Title.

  E230.F67 2013
  973.3'3—dc23   2011048847

Editorial Credits
Mari Bolte, editor; Heidi Thompson, designer; Wanda Winch, media researcher;
Laura Manthe, production specialist

Photo Credits
Alamy: North Wind Picture Archives, 8, 12, 21, 29; Bridgeman Images: Don
Troiani, 7, 10, 17, 25; Courtesy of Army Art Collection: U.S. Army History
Center of Military History, 28; Dreamstime: Flavijus, 5 (inset map); Getty
Images: Bettmann, 15, 20; Library of Congress: Prints and Photographs Division,
9, 19; National Parks Service: Colonial National Historical Park/Sidney E. King,
27; White Historic Art: Pamela Patrick White, www.ppatrickwhite.com, 23

Printed in the United States   5188

Table of Contents

Direct quotations appear on the following pages:
Page 12, from *The Army and Navy of America* by Jacob K. Neff
(Philadelphia, J. H. Persol & Co., 1845.)
Page 25, from *Another Such Victory: The Story of the American Defeat
at Guilford Courthouse That Helped Win the War for Independence*
by Thomas E. Baker (New York: Eastern Acorn Press, 1981.)

CHAPTER 1

A Call for War

For years, Great Britain had ruled the 13 American colonies. A war with France for American soil put Great Britain, the victor, in debt. British leaders decided to tax their subjects to pay the debt.

However, many colonists felt the taxes challenged their rights. They formed protests and boycotted British goods. In return, Great Britain's King George III sent troops to the colonies. He also created laws to further control the colonists.

By 1775 the colonists decided to fight for their freedom. A series of battles took place throughout the colonies. Patriots fought Loyalists. Friends fought friends and neighbors fought neighbors. Families, fields, and homes were torn apart. The war became known as the American Revolution.

colony: a place that is settled by people from another country and is controlled by that country

debt: money that a person owes

Biggest Battles of the American Revolution

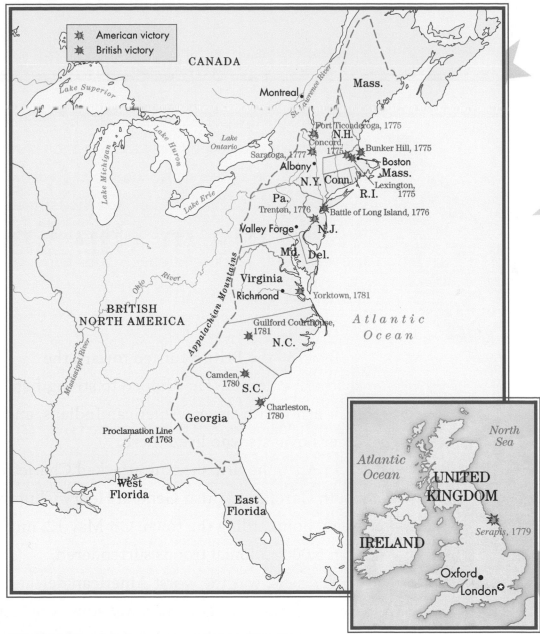

boycott: to refuse to take part in something as a way of making a protest

Loyalist: a colonist who was loyal to Great Britain during the Revolutionary War

CHAPTER 2

Early Battles

Battles of Lexington and Concord
April 18–19, 1775

On the morning of April 18, 1775, the people of Boston, Massachusetts, saw a sea of red. More than 800 British soldiers, also known as Redcoats, lined up outside the town. They marched toward the towns of Lexington and Concord. The plan was to arrest Patriot leaders Samuel Adams and John Hancock in Lexington. Then they would collect Patriot weapons and gunpowder in nearby Concord.

However, the soldiers' march was not a secret. When the British arrived in Lexington, about 70 colonial soldiers stood waiting.

British Major John Pitcairn ordered the Patriots to move out of the way. Moments later, a musket shot was fired. The British assumed a colonist was the shooter and fired back. When the smoke cleared, 18 colonists were wounded or dead.

FAST FACTS The "shot heard 'round the world" inspired people across the globe to stand up to unfair governments.

During the Battles of Lexington and Concord, 273 British soldiers and 95 colonists were killed.

Discovering that Adams and Hancock had escaped, the soldiers moved on to Concord. There they destroyed weapons and gunpowder, creating a huge fire. Patriot Minutemen thought Concord was on fire and moved to defend the town. Surprised, the British retreated.

Colonists chased the British 20 miles (32 kilometers) back to Boston. Militiamen hid in the forest, shooting at the British soldiers' bright red coats as they marched by. Colonists from around Lexington and Concord joined in the battle. Musket smoke filled the air.

By the end of the day, the Redcoats were trapped in Boston. British leaders were worried. Before the battle, they never imagined the colonists would fight back. Now they knew the colonists were ready to fight with their lives.

The British soldiers fought in formal, disciplined groups. They were not prepared for the colonists' surprise attacks.

militiamen: a group of volunteer citizens who serve as soldiers in emergencies

Capture of Fort Ticonderoga
May 10, 1775

After the Battles of Lexington and Concord, the colonial army realized it had a big problem. The British army was trapped in Boston. However, the colonial army was short on weapons. The British army needed more soldiers and reinforcements. The two armies were at a draw.

Patriot leaders Ethan Allen and Benedict Arnold planned a raid on Fort Ticonderoga. The fort was lightly guarded and had many large guns.

Early on May 10, a small group of militiamen stormed Fort Ticonderoga. The handful of British soldiers at the fort were still asleep. It was an easy Patriot victory. More than 80 guns and mortars were collected and moved to Boston. The colonists were now able to match the British firepower.

Ethan Allen (top of the steps) and Patriot troops capturing Fort Ticonderoga

Battle of Bunker Hill
June 17, 1775

While Fort Ticonderoga fell, the British were busy in Boston. They built defensive walls and placed artillery high on the hills overlooking Boston. They planned on adding Breed's Hill in nearby Charlestown to their defensive sites.

The colonists also wanted the hill. Early on June 16, 1775, 1,000 Minutemen began fortifying the location. They built fences, trenches, and dirt walls.

Around 3:00 p.m., 2,200 British soldiers attacked. Their progress was slow. The colonists' fortifications were effective. And the soldiers were weighted down by heavy equipment.

The colonists killed more than 1,000 British soldiers, including 100 officers, during the Battle of Bunker Hill.

artillery: cannons and other large guns used during battles

fortify: to construct walls or buildings built for military defenses

The Patriots were able to stop the British not once, but twice. Angered, the British generals charged again. They used fresh soldiers who carried only what they needed to attack.

The British soldiers were determined. The Patriots began running out of ammunition. Finally they were overwhelmed. Two hours after the battle started, the British won.

Technically the Battle of Bunker Hill is considered a British victory. But the British had three times the number of casualties as the Patriots. The British lost more men in this battle than in any other fought during the war. This battle helped the colonists see that it was possible to beat the British.

Two Hills, One Name

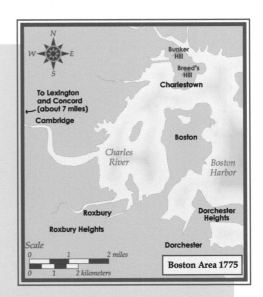

There were actually two hills outside Boston—Breed's Hill and Bunker Hill. Historians don't know why the colonists chose to fortify Breed's Hill. Bunker Hill would have been a better choice. It was taller and farther away from the British artillery. It is believed that the battle is named for Bunker Hill because that was the location originally targeted.

Battle of Long Island
August 22–29, 1776

After the victory at Breed's Hill, the British were able to hold Boston until late 1775. But they now knew the colonists meant to defend themselves. In late June 1775, British General Thomas Gage wrote,

"The rebels are not the despicable rabble too many have supposed them to be."

A painting of the Battle of Long Island

Eventually the British soldiers left Boston. But they were not done fighting. They planned to sail to New York and retake New England. But their plans were discovered. Troops led by General George Washington planned to attack Long Island.

But Washington's men were no match for the British. New York City was an ideal place for Great Britain's navy. The British troops greatly outnumbered Washington's. And their commander, General William Howe, was more experienced.

On August 22, the British ships landed in Long Island. Small groups of Patriots and Redcoats exchanged fire. Four days later, the battle really began. Washington's 9,000 men were no match for the 20,000 Redcoats. The main battle was over in a day, with more than 2,000 colonists lost. If Howe continued the fight, the Continental army would be finished.

Fate was with the Continentals. A heavy, wet fog rolled over the island. Howe decided to wait until the weather cleared before capturing the colonists. On August 29, Washington was able to use the fog's cover to escape.

The battle left the British feeling confident they could defeat the Continental army. In turn, the colonists began to doubt whether they could overcome the Redcoats. Many colonial soldiers began to desert.

FAST FACTS

The Battle of Long Island was the first battle after the Declaration of Independence was signed.

Battle of Trenton
December 26, 1776

It was late in 1776, and morale in the Continental army was low. After a series of defeats, the army was constantly retreating. It seemed as though the war was lost. Many enlisted Continental soldiers were eligible to leave the army at the end of the year. Most planned to return home.

General Washington knew he needed a victory. He came up with a clever but dangerous plan. He would attack German mercenaries, called Hessians, stationed in Trenton, New Jersey.

Washington planned to launch a surprise attack on December 26. In the late afternoon of December 25, Washington and 2,700 men began crossing the Delaware River.

FAST FACTS

Legend has it that the Hessians were tired from holiday festivities. However, evidence suggests that they were exhausted because they had been expecting an attack for more than a week.

The river was icy, and it was raining and snowing heavily. The men arrived several hours later than intended. After the river crossing, the men faced a long, slow march.

enlist: to voluntarily join a branch of the military
mercenary: a soldier who is paid to fight for a foreign army

14

The attack began around 8 a.m. The surprised Hessians fought as best they could. They soon surrendered. This victory raised the spirits of the Continentals. Most of Washington's army re-enlisted at the end of the year.

What's Wrong with This Picture?

In 1851 an artist named Emanuel Leutze painted a picture of Washington crossing the Delaware. However, Leutze had not been at the crossing and didn't know how things had looked at the time. While dramatic, there are a number of historical inaccuracies in this famous painting.

Picture is too bright for the time of day

Washington appears older than he actually was at the time

Clear weather

Betsy Ross flag would not have been carried at this point in the war

Washington is standing dangerously at the front of the boat

Ice is chunky; actual ice on the Delaware would have been flat sheets

Wrong kind of boat; the boats that were used had high sides

Battle of Saratoga
September 19 and October 7, 1777

In September 1777, the British hatched a plan to cut off the northeast colonies. The soldiers would march from Fort Saint-Jean near Lake Champlain along the Hudson River in New York. The army would capture towns and forts in its way. This action would give the British control of both sides of the river. The Continental army would be unable to cross this line to get supplies and soldiers. The British believed this action would win the war.

The Patriot forces near Saratoga, New York, learned of the plan. They prepared for battle by fortifying Bemis Heights, the highest hill in the area.

Thousands of militiamen gathered to fight at Saratoga. Eventually the colonial force at Bemis Heights numbered around 15,000.

Battle of Saratoga

Freeman's Farm

Burgoyne's Headquarters

British Camp

Saratoga National Historical Park

Bemis Heights

American Camp

Hudson River

0   0.5 mile
0   0.5 kilometer

BRITISH NORTH AMERICA

Quebec

Montreal
Fort Saint-Jean

Lake Champlain

Maine (part of Massachusetts)

Burgoyne's Route

Vermont (claimed by New Hampshire and New York)

New Hampshire

Connecticut River

Lake Ontario

Saratoga (see inset)

New York

Massachusetts

Hudson River

Conn.   R.I.

Pennsylvania

New Jersey   Long Island

Atlantic Ocean

0   50   100 miles
0   50   100 kilometers

On September 19, around 8,000 British soldiers set up camp at Loyalist John Freeman's farm. The armies were less than 2 miles (3.2 kilometers) apart, but thick woods stood between them.

Under a heavy fog, British troops made their way toward Bemis Heights. But colonial sharpshooters were hidden in the woods. The sharpshooters were able to kill many British soldiers and officers from the safety of their hiding places. Other Patriot troops charged the British directly. The Redcoats lost about 600 men that day.

The Battle of Saratoga is also known as the Battle of Freeman's Farm.

British General John Burgoyne thought help was coming. He waited three weeks for reinforcements. During this time, many British officers urged him to retreat. But Burgoyne believed he could win. Eventually he realized there would be no reinforcements. He attacked on October 7.

The Patriots were prepared. Muskets and bayonets ready, they charged. They captured British artillery and targeted officers. But despite their early rally, the colonists began to fade. When it looked as though the British were pushing back, Continental General Benedict Arnold rode forward. His shouts to battle inspired the colonists.

Eventually the British soldiers were surrounded. Finally the remaining 6,000 soldiers surrendered on October 14.

Today the Battle of Saratoga is considered the turning point of the war. It proved that the Continental army could win a major battle. This victory convinced France to help the colonists fight the British.

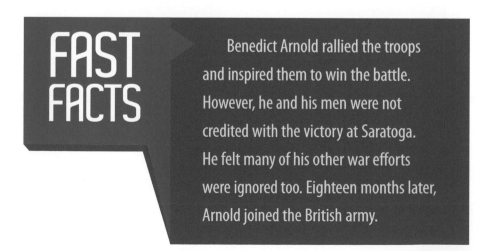

FAST FACTS

Benedict Arnold rallied the troops and inspired them to win the battle. However, he and his men were not credited with the victory at Saratoga. He felt many of his other war efforts were ignored too. Eighteen months later, Arnold joined the British army.

Battle of the *Serapis*
September 23, 1779

For many years, British warships were seen as the most powerful in the world. In an attempt to fight this huge fleet, the Patriots built a navy of privateers. These sailors allowed their personal ships to be used by the Continental army. Colonists hoped these ships would attempt to keep British trade and supply vessels from reaching their intended ports.

Fighting on the water changed after France joined the war. In 1779 colonial Captain John Paul Jones was given command of a French ship called the USS *Bonhomme Richard*. He piloted the ship around Great Britain's coast, seeking British vessels to engage in battle.

John Paul Jones has been called the father of the United States Navy.

privateer: a person who owns a ship licensed to attack and steal from other ships

19

On September 23, 1779, the *Bonhomme Richard* encountered the more powerful HMS *Serapis*. The ships exchanged gunfire, and the *Serapis* easily outclassed the *Bonhomme Richard*. But when the British asked him to surrender, Jones yelled,

"I have not yet begun to fight!"

The Battle of the *Serapis* lasted four hours.

Jones knew that he couldn't win by fighting with guns. He sailed as close as possible to the *Serapis*. Then he ordered the men to board the *Serapis* and engage in close combat. The ships' guns continued to fire at each other. Sharpshooters targeted crewmembers on deck. Grenades were thrown over the deck, causing explosions and fires.

Eventually Jones captured the *Serapis* and her crew. Unfortunately the *Bonhomme Richard* was too damaged to sail. The ship was both flooding and on fire. The *Bonhomme Richard* sank on September 25.

The *Bonhomme Richard* floated for another 36 hours after Jones and his crew abandoned it.

CHAPTER 3

Battles in the South

Siege of Charleston
early April–May 12, 1780

By 1780 the British turned toward the southern colonies. They hoped to strengthen their army with slaves, American Indians, and other Loyalists who lived there.

In April the British army attacked Charleston, South Carolina. British General Henry Clinton began bombarding the town. On May 12, more than 5,000 Colonial troops surrendered.

The siege was the worst American defeat of the revolution. Great Britain was now convinced that they could easily win back the colonies.

What's It Called?

During a seige, a city or fort is completely surrounded. Fortifications are targeted until they break down, making the city easier to attack. The people inside will also eventually run out of food and ammunition. The Battle of Yorktown is sometimes called the Siege of Yorktown.

Battle of Camden
August 16, 1780

A few months later, the two armies met again in nearby Camden. The colonial army was less disciplined and quickly retreated. The British cavalry gave chase, easily overtaking the Patriots. More than 1,000 colonists were killed, and another 1,000 were captured. The British lost only 324 soldiers. Their victory at Camden made it easier for Great Britain to control the Carolinas.

Militiamen at Camden lacked bayonets, which put them at a disadvantage in close combat.

Battle of Guilford Courthouse
March 15, 1781

The British army had won many important victories in the South. But by 1781 the Continental army gained the upper hand. The British had chased the colonists farther than they planned. Their supplies were low. The soldiers were exhausted. The Continentals had worn the British down.

In March British General Lord Charles Cornwallis and 1,900 British soldiers were on the move. They were chasing Colonial General Nathanael Greene and his men through Greensboro, North Carolina. As they marched through a wooded area, they came face-to-face with more than 4,000 of Greene's troops.

The British were completely outmatched. Cornwallis became desperate. He ordered soldiers to fire into the crowded field to stop the fighting. Shots wounded both colonial and British soldiers. Greene withdrew his men.

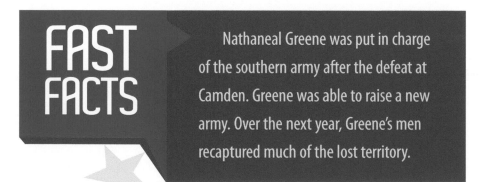

FAST FACTS

Nathaneal Greene was put in charge of the southern army after the defeat at Camden. Greene was able to raise a new army. Over the next year, Greene's men recaptured much of the lost territory.

Although it was a British victory, Cornwallis suffered huge losses. About 500 of his men were killed, including one-third of his officers. After hearing news of the battle, a member of Parliament exclaimed,

"Another such victory would ruin the British army!"

The Battle of Guilford Courthouse lasted two and a half hours.

Cornwallis decided to abandon the Carolinas. Instead, he headed to Yorktown, Virginia. There, he hoped to gather supplies and reinforcements.

CHAPTER 4

The Final Battle

Battle of Yorktown
September 28–October 19, 1781

Yorktown was surrounded by water on three sides. General Cornwallis thought it would be easier to defend. He also expected British supply ships and reinforcements to meet him there. The army could then restock and reform its battle plan.

General Washington planned to trap Cornwallis at Yorktown. He would pretend to lead 7,000 Continental and French soldiers to New York. But instead of going to New York, they would head to Yorktown. He hoped his plan would prevent Cornwallis from calling for reinforcements.

Around this time, Washington also received a letter from French Admiral Comte de Grasse. The admiral would lend his fleet of ships to assist Washington.

On September 4, de Grasse's ships arrived in Yorktown. The fleet was able to drive off the 19 British ships in the harbor. Cornwallis would not be able to add to his army of 8,000. He would also not be able to leave Yorktown by ship.

Washington's headquarters at Yorktown

By the beginning of October, almost 20,000 Patriot and French troops were stationed outside Yorktown. They had more than 50 large guns pointed at the enemy. They vowed to stay until the British surrendered.

Only a few minor battles occurred. The Patriots held their ground. Cornwallis couldn't escape. He surrendered on October 17, 1781.

Without reinforcements, Cornwallis' army was unable to defeat the Patriots.

I Surrender!

General Cornwallis felt embarrassed losing to the colonists. He sent Charles O'Hara, his second-in-command, to surrender in his place, claiming to be ill.

When O'Hara tried to deliver Cornwallis' sword as a sign of surrender, he was rejected twice—once by a French general and once by Washington. Finally he gave the sword to Major General Benjamin Lincoln—Washington's second-in-command.

The Battle of Yorktown proved the final blow for the British. Although King George III wanted to continue fighting, his military leaders did not. They convinced the king to end the Revolutionary War.

The Treaty of Paris was signed on September 3, 1783, recognizing the United States of America as a country. All Great Britain's land in the 13 colonies now belonged to the United States.

A ceremony was held on October 19, 1781. There, the British officially surrendered to Washington (center).

treaty: an official agreement between two or more groups or countries

Glossary

artillery (ar-TI-luhr-ee)—cannons and other large guns used during battles

boycott (BOY-kot)—to refuse to take part in something as a way of making a protest

colony (KAH-luh-nee)—a place that is settled by people from another country and is controlled by that country

debt (DET)—money that a person owes

desert (di-ZUHRT)—to leave military service without permission

enlist (en-LIST)—to voluntarily join a branch of the military

fortify (FOR-tuh-fye)—to construct walls or buildings to be used as military defenses

Loyalist (LOI-uh-list)—a colonist who was loyal to Great Britain during the Revolutionary War

mercenary (MUR-suh-nayr-ee)—a soldier who is paid to fight for a foreign army

militiamen (muh-LISH-uh)—a group of volunteer citizens who serve as soldiers in emergencies

Minutemen (MIH-nuht-men)—colonists who were ready and willing to fight at a moment's notice

Patriot (PAY-tree-uht)—a person who sided with the colonies during the Revolutionary War

privateer (prye-vuh-TEER)—a person who owns a ship licensed to attack and steal from other ships

treaty (TREE-tee)—an official agreement between two or more groups or countries

Read More

Burgan, Michael. *Weapons, Gear, and Uniforms of the American Revolution*. Equipped for Battle. Mankato, Minn.: Capstone Press, 2012.

Gregory, Josh. *The Revolutionary War*. Cornerstones of Freedom. New York: Children's Press, 2012.

Samuels, Charlie. *Timeline of the Revolutionary War*. Americans at War. New York: Gareth Stevens Pub., 2012.

Internet Sites

FactHound offers a safe, fun way to find Internet sites related to this book. All of the sites on FactHound have been researched by our staff.

Here's all you do:

Visit *www.facthound.com*

Type in this code: 9781429684293

Super-cool stuff! Check out projects, games and lots more at **www.capstonekids.com**

Index